# ZOMBIE FUNNIES

By Daryle Conners

an imprint of
**SCHOLASTIC**
www.scholastic.com

Published by Tangerine Press, an imprint of Scholastic Inc., 557 Broadway, New York, NY 10012
Scholastic Canada, Ltd., Markham, Ontario
Scholastic New Zealand Ltd., Greenmount, Auckland

Scholastic and Tangerine Press and associated logos are trademarks and/or registered trademarks of Scholastic Inc.

becker&mayer!
BOOK PRODUCERS

*Zombie Funnies* is produced by becker&mayer!
11120 NE 33rd Place, Suite 101
Bellevue, WA 98004
www.beckermayer.com

ISBN: 978-0-545-57258-3

10 9 8 7 6 5 4 3 2 1    13 14 15 16 17
12652

Editor: Ben Grossblatt
Designer: Brandon Walker
Photo Researcher: Emily Zach
Production Coordinator: Diane Ross
Product Developer: Peter Schumacher
Managing Editor: Nicole Burns Ascue
Additional material written by Tyler Freidenrich

**Q: Why did the zombie stop teaching?**

*A: He only had one pupil!*

**Q: What did the zombie say when he ate the comedian?**

*A: "This tastes funny!"*

**Q: Why did the zombie get expelled from school?**

*A: He kept buttering up his teacher!*

**Q: What do zombies call bicyclists?**

*A: Meals on wheels!*

**Knock knock!**

*Who's there?*

**Interrupting zombie.**

*Interrup-*

**Braaains!**

**Q: What goes "Sniaaarb! Sniaaarb!"?**

*A: A zombie in reverse!*

**Q: What do you call a friendly, handsome zombie?**

*A: A total failure!*

**Q: What is the difference between a zombie and a birthday candle?**

*A: The candle is about 100 times brighter!*

**WARNING ZOMBIE OUTBREAK LEAVE THE CITY**

**Q: What do you call dead cows that come back to life?**

*A: Zombeef!*

**Q: Why did the zombie keep arguing?**

A: Because he knew he was dead right!

**Q: Why could the zombie sleep through the noisy party?**

A: Because he was dead to the world!

**Q: Why did the zombie live alone?**

A: He was fed up with other people!

Q: Why did the zombie eat the tightrope walker?

A: He wanted a balanced meal!

Q: What is zombie Mozart doing these days?

A: Decomposing!

Q: How do you help a hungry zombie?

A: Just give him a helping hand!

**Q: What's a zombie's favorite Italian food?**

*A: Pete-za!*

**Q: What did the zombies eat at the picnic?**

*A: Barbara-que!*

ZOMBIE
OUTBREAK
QUARANTINE
AREA

**Q: What did everyone say about the zombie movie star?**

*A: "She's drop-dead gorgeous!"*

**Q: Why did people always mistake the zombie for his brother?**

*A: Because they were dead ringers!*

**Q: What does it take to become a zombie?**

*A: Lots of dead-ication!*

**Q: What do you call a confused zombie?**

*A: Scatterbrained!*

**Q: Who did the zombie take out for dinner?**

*A: His ghoulfriend!*

**Q: What did the zombie say before his fight?**

*A: "Do you want a piece of me?"*

**Q: Why do zombies hate going to the beach?**

*A: Too many lifeguards!*

**Q: What do zombies call sprinters?**

*A: Fast food!*

**Q: What do you call a zombie who eats his uncle's wife?**

*A: An aunt-eater!*

**Q: What's the best way to talk to a zombie?**

*A: From very far away!*

**Q: What do they serve for lunch at zombie school?**

A: Human beans, sloppy toes, and eyes cream!

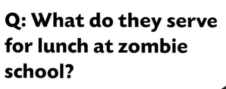

**Q: Why did the zombie act crazy?**

A: Because he lost his head!

**Q: What's the best way to escape from zombie pirates?**

A: In a lifeboat!

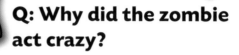

**Q: What do you call a zombie chicken?**

*A: A poultry-geist!*

**Q: What did the zombie throw off the boat?**

*A: All the life jackets!*

**Q: What's a zombie's favorite kind of puzzle?**

*A: A brainteaser!*

**Q: What did the zombie say to her new boyfriend?**

A: "You've stolen my heart!"

**Q: What kind of TV does a zombie have?**

A: A wide-scream TV!

**Q: Who won the zombie soccer game?**

A: No one. It was dead even!

**Q: What's a zombie girl's favorite kind of guy?**

A: The brainy kind!

**Q: When do zombies leave the dinner table?**

A: After everyone's eaten!

**Q: How do zombies keep burglars out?**

A: With deadbolt locks!

**Q: What did the mixed-up zombie eat?**

*A: Some guy named Brian!*

**Q: What do you call a very determined zombie?**

*A: A diehard!*

**Q: What did the zombie text right before he died?**

*A: BRB!*

**Q: What do you call zombies who like bad jokes?**

*A: The pun-dead!*

**Q: What musical instruments do zombies like best?**

*A: Organs!*

**Q: Why did the zombie want to go to Harvard?**

*A: She heard that's where the best brains were!*

**Q: Why was the zombie afraid of the jury?**

*A: He thought they'd give him a life sentence!*

**Q: Why isn't the zombie restaurant popular?**

*A: Because dinner costs an arm and a leg!*

**Q: What does a zombie get when he comes home late for dinner?**

*A: The cold shoulder!*

RED POINT WARNING
INFECTED PEOPLE NOT ALLOWED

**Q: Why wouldn't the zombie cross the road?**

*A: Because he had no guts!*

**Q: What did the zombie parents say to their kid before her school play?**

*A: "Knock 'em dead!"*

**Q: What position does a zombie play in hockey?**

*A: Ghoulie!*

**Q: Why didn't the zombie guy marry the human girl?**

A: Because his family was dead set against it!

**Q: Who did the unpopular zombie invite to his party?**

A: Everyone he could dig up!

**Q: What did the zombie dad say when his teenage son asked to borrow the car?**

A: "Over my dead body!"

**Q: Who won the zombie 100-yard dash?**

*A: No one. It was a dead heat!*

**Q: Why did the zombie racecar driver quit?**

*A: There was too much life in the fast lane!*

**Q: Why did the zombie employees eat the company president?**

*A: Because he was the brains of the operation!*

**Q: What's a zombie's favorite play?**

A: Romeo and Ghouliet!

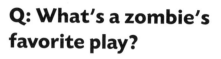

**Q: What was the zombie dog's best trick?**

A: Roll over and play alive!

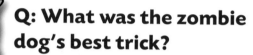

**Q: What did the grandfather zombie say to his zombie grandson?**

A: "You gruesome."

**Q: What do you call a graveyard romance?**

*A: Boy meets ghoul!*

**Q: Where do baby zombies go while their parents are at work?**

*A: Day-scare!*

**Q: What do zombie kids play on the playground?**

*A: Hide and Shriek!*

EMERGENCY

BITTEN PEOPLE
WILL NOT
BE ADMITTED

ZOMBIE
OUTBREAK

**Q: Why did the zombies put a wall around the cemetery?**

A: Because people were dying to get in!

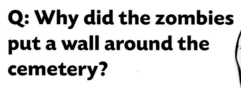

**Q: Why are zombies so forgetful?**

A: Because everything goes in one ear and out the other!

**Q: Where did the zombie keep her snacks?**

A: In her handbag!

**Q: What did the zombie say when he saw a train full of passengers?**

A: "Oh, yummy. A chew-chew train!"

**Q: What did the zombie do when his hand fell off?**

A: He went to a secondhand shop!

**Q: What did the zombie serve for appetizers?**

A: Finger food!

**Q: What's a zombie's favorite fast food?**

*A: Handburgers!*

**Q: What makes a zombie really mad?**

*A: That's a no-brainer!*

**Q: How do you catch a zombie?**

*A: With a deathtrap!*

**Q: What do you call a serious zombie?**

A: A very grave guy!

**Q: What did the zombie say to his blind date?**

A: "I've been dying to meet you!"

**Q: What do you call zombie kids' recess games?**

A: Foul play!

**Q: What did the zombie mother say to her kids at dinnertime?**

A: "Don't talk with someone in your mouth!"

WARNING ZOMBIE ATTACKS IN THIS AREA

**Q: What happened to Ray after he met a zombie?**

A: He became an ex-Ray!

**Q: What did the zombie say to his friend?**

A: "I need some advice. Can I pick your brain?"

**Q: Why didn't the football team like playing against the zombies?**

A: Because they always went into sudden death!

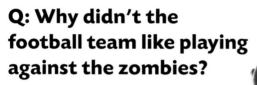

**Q: Why did the zombie sleep so much?**

A: Because he was dead tired!

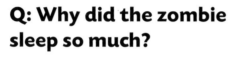

**Q: What is the difference between zombies and torn jeans?**

A: Zombies are dead men, and torn jeans are men-ded!

**Q: How do American zombies serve their country?**

A: In the U.S. Marine Corpse!

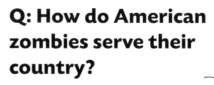

**Q: Why did the zombie lawyer lose his case?**

A: Because he didn't have a leg to stand on!

**Q: What do you call a zombie with kids?**

A: A momster!

**Q: What happened when the zombies heard the shocking news?**

*A: There was a dead silence!*

**Q: Why was the zombie kicked off the swim team?**

*A: Because he was dead in the water!*

**Q: Where does a zombie like to sleep?**

*A: On her deathbed!*

WARNING
ZOMBIES
AHEAD!!!

**Q: Why didn't the zombies care when their arms and legs fell off?**

A: Because they wanted to rest in pieces!

**Q: What did the zombie mom say to her son at dinner?**

A: "Junior, don't leave your elbow on the table."

**Q: Why did the zombie always carry a bottle of ketchup?**

A: In case he ran into an old friend!

**Q: How did the zombie get so brainy?**

*A: You know what they say—"You are what you eat!"*

**Q: What do healthy zombies eat?**

*A: Whole-brain bread!*

**Q: How did the zombie get from New York to Los Angeles?**

*A: He took a nonstop fright!*

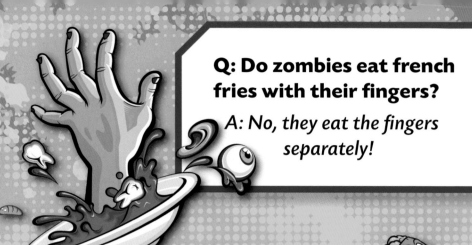

**Q: Do zombies eat french fries with their fingers?**

*A: No, they eat the fingers separately!*

**Q: What do you call a bunch of zombies all in a row?**

*A: A deadline!*

**Q: During a zombie attack, where's the safest place to hide?**

*A: The living room!*

SAFETY GUARANTEE
ZOMBIE PROOF

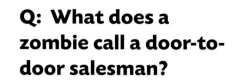

**Q: What does a zombie call a door-to-door salesman?**

*A: Dinner!*

**Q: What's a zombie's favorite day of the week?**

*A: Moan-day!*

**Q: Where do zombies go swimming?**

*A: In the Dead Sea!*

WARNING ZOMBIES AHEAD

LEAVE THIS AREA

**Q: What do you call it when a zombie cleans up after dinner?**

A: *Brainwashing!*

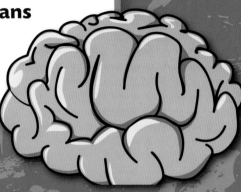

**Q: Why did the zombie put his head on the piano keys?**

A: *Because he was trying to play by ear!*

**Q: How are zombies like computers?**

A: *They've both got lots of mega-bites!*

**Q: Where did the zombie take out a loan?**

A: *The blood bank!*

**Q: Why did the zombie go to the hospital?**

A: *He wanted to learn a few sick jokes!*

**GREEN AREA**
**ZOMBIE FREE**
WOUNDED PEOPLE
NOT ALLOWED

**Q: What do polite zombies say when they're introduced to someone new?**

A: *"Pleased to eat you."*

**Q: Why didn't the zombie get married?**

*A: He just couldn't meet the right ghoul!*

**Q: What happened to the zombie who ate a sheep?**

*A: He felt baaad!*

**Q: How are zombies like false teeth?**

*A: They all come out at night!*

**Q: What do zombies like on their sundaes?**

*A: Whipped scream!*

**Q: Why didn't the zombie go to the drive-thru?**

*A: Because he didn't like fast food!*

**Q: Why are zombie parties so dull?**

*A: Because no one can be the life of the party!*

**Q: Did you hear about the zombie whose left arm and left leg fell off?**

A: He's all right now!

**Q: What kind of coffee do zombies drink?**

A: De-coffinated!

**Q: Where do zombies shop?**

A: At the gross-ery store!

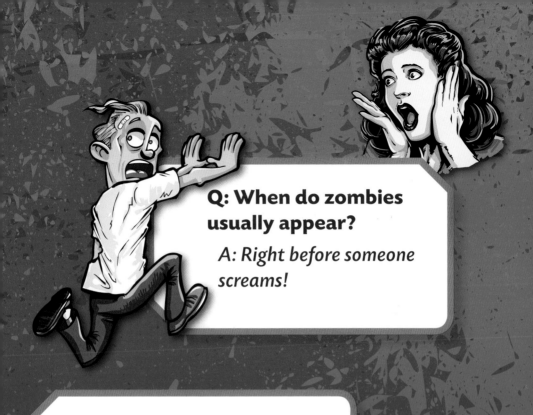

**Q: When do zombies usually appear?**

A: Right before someone screams!

**Q: What do you call someone who hangs out with zombies?**

A: A numbskull!

**Q: What did the zombie say to the stranger?**

A: "I'd really like to get to gnaw you!"

**Q: Why did the zombie sit down?**

A: Because he was dead on his feet!

**Q: What do zombies like best about baseball?**

A: The doubleheaders!

**Q: What kind of trees do zombies like best?**

A: Ceme-trees!

**Q: What's the hardest thing to sell a zombie?**

*A: Life insurance!*

**Q: What kind of horse does a zombie ride?**

*A: A nightmare!*

**Q: How do zombies celebrate New Year's Eve?**

*A: They paint the town dead!*

**Q: What did the zombie eat after he got his tooth pulled?**

A: The dentist!

**Q: Why do little zombies go to school?**

A: To get deaducated!

**Q: Why wouldn't the zombie's car start?**

A: Dead battery!

**Q: What do you call a zombie's neighborhood?**

*A: His terror-tory!*

**Q: Did you hear about the zombie who tried to live on rabbits?**

*A: It was a hare-brained scheme!*

**Q: What kind of gems do zombies wear?**

*A: Tombstones!*

**Q: What cereal does a zombie eat for breakfast?**

A: Raisin Braaain!

**Q: What did the man say to the zombie?**

A: "Get a life!"

**Q: What does a vampire crossed with a zombie say?**

A: "Veeeeins!"

**Q: What's a zombie's favorite direction?**

A: *Dead ahead!*

**Q: What's a zombie's favorite position in basketball?**

A: *Dead center!*

**Q: What kind of weather do zombies dream about?**

A: *Brainstorms!*

**Q: What was the slogan of the zombie restaurant?**

A: "A Mind Is a Wonderful Thing to Taste"

**Q: How do zombies smooth the ice at the hockey rink?**

A: They use a Zomboni!

**Q: What do you call someone who believes all the latest zombie rumors?**

A: Ghoulable!

**Q: What kind of candy do zombies refuse to eat?**

*A: Life Savers!*

**Q: How did the zombie win the football game?**

*A: He carried the ball over the ghoul line!*

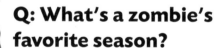

**Q: What's a zombie's favorite season?**

*A: The dead of winter!*

**Q: Where do you buy zombies?**

A: At the monstore!

**Q: Why couldn't the zombie teams finish the game?**

A: They were hopelessly deadlocked!

**Q: What is a zombie's favorite band?**

A: The Grateful Dead!

**Q: Why was the zombie so heavy to carry?**

A: *He was dead weight!*

**Q: What do you call a lazy zombie?**

A: *A deadbeat!*

**Q: What were the zombie kids doing at the playground?**

A: *Playing Swallow the Leader!*

**Q: What do you call a famous zombie?**

*A: A monstar!*

**Q: What did the zombie say after eating the man's brain?**

*A: "Thanks for the memories!"*

**Q: What's a zombie's favorite kind of boat?**

*A: A blood vessel!*

**Q: Why didn't the zombie go to the party?**

*A: He felt rotten!*

**Q: How do you stop a zombie from smelling?**

*A: Pull off his nose!*

**Q: What should you do if a zombie comes to your front door?**

*A: Run out the back door!*

**Q: Why did the man want to be a zombie?**

*A: Because the cost of living was too high!*

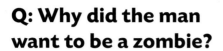

**Q: What goes ha-ha-ha-thud?**

*A: A zombie laughing his head off!*

**Q: What is a little zombie's favorite toy?**

*A: A deady bear!*

**Q: Why did the zombie teenager hide her old dress?**

*A: Because she wouldn't be caught dead in it!*

**Q: Where do zombies live?**

*A: On dead-end streets!*

DEAD END

**Q: What do you do if you see a zombie?**

*A: Hope it's actually Halloween!*

**Q: What do you call a dead bumblebee?**

*A: A zom-bee!*

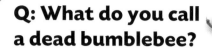

**Q: How do zombies predict the future?**

*A: They check their horrorscopes!*

**Q: What happens when zombies go to the theater?**

*A: The actors all get stage fright!*

**BEWARE** OF **ZOMBIES**

**Q: What do you call a zombie who only eats human flesh?**

*A: A humanitarian!*

**Q: What do you call a zombie bargain?**

*A: A dead giveaway!*

**Q: What did the zombie's party invitation say?**

*A: "The morgue the merrier!"*

WARNING ZOMBIES AHEAD LEAVE THIS AREA

**Q: What did the zombie say when he was full?**

A: "I'm stuffed! I couldn't eat another mortal!"

**Q: Who does the Big Bad Zombie Wolf eat?**

A: Little Dead Riding Hood!

ZOMBIE
OUTBREAK
INFECTED
AREA

**Q: Where did the zombie go for a cruise?**

A: The Deaditerranean Sea!

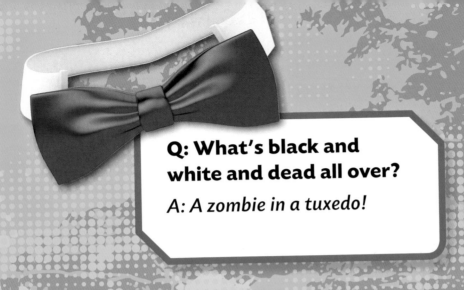

**Q: What's black and white and dead all over?**

*A: A zombie in a tuxedo!*

**Doctor: Are you still having trouble with your breathing?**

*Zombie: Yes, I am.*

**Doctor: Let's see if we can put a stop to that!**

**Q: Why did the zombie refuse to buy the new appliance?**

*A: Because it was guaranteed for life!*

**Q: What has four legs and flies?**

*A: Two zombies!*

**Q: What did the zombie eat at the dinner party?**

*A: All the guests!*

**Q: What did the zombie eat when he ordered take-out?**

*A: The delivery man!*

**Q: What does a zombie dog eat?**

*A: The hand that used to feed him!*

**Q: What do zombie kids love to eat?**

*A: Mike and cheese!*

**Q: What did the zombie bring to the blood drive?**

*A: A mug!*

**Knock knock!**

*Who's there?*

**Unnnnggh.**

*Unnnnggh who?*

**Unnnnggh urrrggh!**

**Q: What do zombies like to eat around the campfire?**

*A: Franks and Bens!*

**Q: What did the zombie eat for lunch?**

*A: A Sam-wich!*

**Q: What does a zombie call *People* magazine?**

A: A menu!

**Q: How did the zombie invite his zombie friend to go watch a basketball game?**

A: "Want to go to the food court?"

**Q: Why don't zombie kids play with human kids?**

A: Because they know they're not supposed to play with their food!